Maldon's Scripture Guide: A Practice Manual

Shawn Maldon, M.Ed-IP, NIC
Maldon Language Interpreters, LLC
www.MaldonInterpreting.com

MALDON'S SCRIPTURE GUIDE: A PRACTICE MANUAL

Shawn Maldon, M.Ed-IP, NIC

© Copyright 2023 by Shawn Maldon

ALL RIGHTS RESERVED. No part of this product may be modified or altered in any form whatsoever, electronic, or mechanical, including photocopying, recording, or by any informational storage or retrieval system without express written, dated and signed permission from the author.

DISCLAIMER AND/OR LEGAL NOTICES: The information presented herein represents the view of the author as of the date of publication. Because of the rate with which information changes, the author reserves the right to alter and update his opinion based on new conditions. The book is for informational purposes only. While every attempt has been made to verify the information provided, neither the author nor his affiliates/partners assume any responsibility for errors, inaccuracies or omissions. Any slights of people or organizations are unintentional. If advice concerning legal or related matters is needed, the services of a fully qualified professional should be sought. This book is not intended for use as a source of legal advice. You should be aware of any laws which govern practices in your country and state. Any reference to any person or business, whether living or dead, is purely coincidental.

ISBN: 979-8-9882471-0-4

Publisher:	The Maldon Brand 1202 Castlehaven Court Capitol Heights, MD 20743
Contact:	www.ShawnMaldon.com Maldon@ShawnMaldon.com
Cover Design:	Glenda Kelly
Training Handout Design:	Amanda Anderson

This is my first book (hopefully not my last). Understandably, I wanted my dedication page to be well thought out, to be impactful. I was going to dedicate it to someone in my immediate family, like maybe my amazing father, Robert Maldon, Sr. However, my mother, Peaches McClure, has always been my rock; yet, my siblings mean the world to me: Dr. Michelle, Robert Jr., and Patrick. Then of course, there is my Godmother who nursed me back to health when I was nearly lifeless and on my sick bed, Glenda Kelly.

I couldn't decide. I guess I will have to write more books after all and give each of them their own dedication page. Let's see that's how many books. I think I counted five.

This time I made the decision to dedicate this book to the American Deaf Community (ADC) as a whole. They have always embraced me and showed me love! In some of my lowest moments, it was a member of the ADC that wrapped their arms around me and comforted me. Furthermore, it's because of them that I have enjoyed a long, profitable, and rewarding career as a Nationally Certified American Sign Language interpreter. I will continue to, not only, help others learning by teaching; I will also always work on my own skill development. I want to get it as right as I can for YOU.

Thank you!

MALDON'S SCRIPTURE GUIDE: A PRACTICE MANUAL

FOREWARD BY
Minister Clarey Walker
Greater Mt. Calvary Holy Church
Washington, DC

As an ordained minister of the Gospel and an interpreter—for nearly two decades—primarily working in religious settings, I am thoroughly impressed with Maldon's Scripture Guide. Outside of the preacher, the ASL interpreter is the most important link in the service as he bridges the gap between the soul of an individual and salvation.

The Bible declares that we must "rightly divide the Word of truth" (2 Timothy 2:15). Just as a preacher has the responsibility of appropriately transmitting meaning from a scripture through hermeneutics and exegesis, so, too, must the interpreter go through the painstaking process to ensure the parishioners fully access the Word. From that translation, they will make decisions that equate to everlasting life for them.

Maldon builds the case for the interpreter to spot relationships within (and outside) the text. Whether one considers the relationship between Biblical characters, the parishioner and Christ, or between the interpreter and the scripture, the identification of relationships is helpful.

As a man of the cloth (and as an ever-growing interpreter), very poignantly for me, Maldon teaches on the importance of each interpreter examining himself. They must self-assess, take inventory, and realize the act of interpreting is not only about them; In religious settings, it is a service unto God that has the ability to draw people to Christ.

MALDON'S SCRIPTURE GUIDE: A PRACTICE MANUAL

Table of Contents

INTRODUCTION..8

KEY TERMINOLOGY...10

CHECK YOUR UNDERSTANDING....................................16

I: READ...19

II: RELATE...23

III: RENDER...31

TRAINING HANDOUT..35

REFERENCES..37

INTRODUCTION

We begin with the end in mind. The goal is to provide accurate scripture translation. While reading the introduction, ask yourself, "What is my purpose?" Is it self-serving? Or is it to learn how to provide a better product for consumers? If you remember your goal, then it will help you proceed, especially when the task at-hand seems daunting. You can do this. Good luck!

American Sign Language interpreting (and/or translating) is a complex process. For it to be done well, there are many aspects of the work to consider. Interpreting in a religious setting, for even some advanced interpreters, can be overwhelming. One can only imagine the challenge for novice interpreters. Maldon's Scripture Guide (MSG) takes the stance that religious interpreting (and/or scripture translating) is perhaps the most challenging of all work that an interpreter might do. This is because of the complexity involved, but also because of the high-stakes nature of the work. Translating the content of a time-old document, like the Bible, presents several challenges. For example, the Bible contains ancient language, different versions, and has been translated to and from more languages than any other document. It's rich in parable, metaphor, dual meanings, and not to mention the various genres within the Bible: personal letters, historical accounts, law, poetry, songs, wisdom literature, apocalyptic writings, and prophesy—just to name a few.

More importantly, the Bible is not just some book full of interesting literary devices. Its purpose is to offer guidance to mankind; it deals with peoples' soul. Unfortunately, there is a lacuna in the research, training and the development of interpreters working in such settings.

Maldon's Scripture Guide: The Practice Manual was created to provide practical skills development as it relates to scripture translations. The most important thing to remember is that the interpreter has a duty to "do no harm." What does this mean? It means that it would be better for the interpreter to be transparent and direct with the consumer(s), than to try and pretend they have the interpreting/translating process under control. If presented with a concept, utterance, or a scripture that the interpreter is not able to transfer meaningfully into the target language, then let the consumer(s) know. 'Do no harm' speaks to not causing the consumers to have a less than favorable perspective of the Bible (since the purpose of this guide is to provide skill development opportunities for translating scriptures). For example, what we do not want is for something that the interpreter unclearly translates to leave the Deaf person saying, "The Bible is confusing, contradictory, vague, and consistently unclear." If the interpreter does not disclose his or her inadequacies, they might jeopardize the meaningfulness of the scripture. Actually, it may not be the Bible, but the interpreter's skillset. I don't know about you, but I do not want 'that blood on my hands' (pun intended).

Allow MSG to provide you with a step-by-step guide to follow. With practice, you can go into a setting where you will do scripture translating and meaning transfer, successfully. First, let's review some key terminology.

MALDON'S SCRIPTURE GUIDE: A PRACTICE MANUAL

KEY TERMINOLOGY

"Learning words is great, but it's even better if you use them."
~Shawn Maldon

These terms are vital to how professionals talk about and understand the work. Take a moment to look up each reference provided at the end of this book. After each key terminology, there are lines. Expand your knowledge. Add additional notes to help you clarify the meaning of the term.

1. **Interpretation**-Working with two languages where both are not written, but spoken and/or signed. Interpreting is the act of conveying meaning between people who use signed and/or spoken languages (RID Motion C2019. 14)

   _____
   _____
   _____
   _____
   _____
   _____

2. **Translation**-Working with two languages where, at least, one is written. Translating consists in reproducing in the receptor language to the closest natural equivalent of the source-language message, first in terms of meaning and secondly in terms of style (Nida 1969).

   _____
   _____
   _____
   _____
   _____
   _____

3. **Time Shifted Meaning Transfer (TSMT)**-Consecutive Interpreting (or TSMT) is defined as the process of interpreting after the speaker or signer has completed one or more ideas in the source language and pauses while the interpreter transmits the information (Russell 2005).

___

___

___

___

___

___

4. **Real Time Meaning Transfer (RTMT)**-Simultaneous Interpreting (or RTMT) is defined as the process of interpreting into the target language at the same time the source language is being delivered (Russell 2005).

___

___

___

___

___

___

5. **Chunking/Organizing the source text**-Chunking refers to organizing the source into manageable limits before starting to interpret (Gonzalez 1991).

___

___

___

6. **Processing Time**-Processing Time refers to the time interpreters use to sufficiently understand a message before interpreting (Boinis 1996).

7. **Constructed Action**-Constructed Action is the use of body, head, and eye gaze, to report the actions, thoughts, words, and expressions of characters within a discourse (Metzger 1995).

8. **Frozen Register**-Frozen Register is static language that is always rendered the same (Humphrey 1994).

9. **Source Language Text (SLT)**-SLT is the text a translator is given to translate into another language (in other words, the original text or the text you start with).

10. **Target Language Text (TLT)**-TLT is the translation of the source text (in other words, the final text or the text you end up with).

CHECK YOUR UNDERSTANDING

You are already smarter. Congratulations! Now, take a moment to solidify what you've learned.

MALDON'S SCRIPTURE GUIDE: A PRACTICE MANUAL

1) What is the difference between an **interpretation** and a **translation**?

_____
_____
_____
_____
_____
_____

2) What is the difference between **TSMT** and **processing time**?

_____
_____
_____
_____
_____
_____

3) To perform interpretation/translation, the **source language text** must always be written.

   TRUE
   FALSE

4) While performing the ASL feature **constructed action**, the interpreter can only assume the role of another person (not an animal).

   TRUE
   FALSE

5) Which of the following is an example of frozen register?

    a. The National Anthem
    b. A familiar sermon (the pastor preaches often)

CHAPTER I: READ

  Once I worked an assignment at a church. I had never worked with this particular interpreter before. She was eager to "interpret." She was slated to interpret the scripture. The pastor read the scripture, "And when they came to Chidon's threshing floor, Uzza put out his hand to hold the ark, for the oxen stumbled," (1 Chronicles 13:9).

  The interpreter got stuck at "threshing floor." She signed PUNCH + FLOOR. Then, she froze. I had to replace her. While she was responsible for the scripture, I still read it. Lesson #1 (and we haven't even started): Get the scripture and READ!

The first step of MSG is to "READ the scripture." First, let's discuss the obvious. If you are to read the scripture, you have to actually look up or get the scripture—in hand. That action alone is not only paramount, but it's also 90% of the translation work. Fortunately, in many religious settings, the interpreter has the opportunity to get the scripture in advance of it being presented. This is key. One of the most important pieces of the puzzle is being able to prepare. Having the scripture ahead of time allows the interpreter to prepare. Many interpreters have "grown up in the church." Sometimes, and when the interpreter does not work professionally, the interpreter may feel that he or she knows the Bible well-enough and does not need to prepare. MSG serves as a reminder of the importance of preparing for the job ahead. Get the scripture, look it up. If followed, MSG will guide the interpreter in reading the scripture a total of four times prior to performing the work.

The guide's first step is for the interpreter to passively read the scripture. What is passive reading? Passive reading is the process of reading shallowly, without putting too much effort into the activity, focusing on the text and comprehension, and actually passing through the material mechanically. In grade school, lots of emphasis was placed on active reading or reading for comprehension. Therefore, here are some tips for how to read passively:

1) Read without doing any pre-reading analysis or contextualization of the scripture
2) Read without questions in mind
3) Read without adjusting to the scripture's content (slower versus faster for more dense content: just read as you normally would)
4) Read without taking notes
5) Read without highlighting, marking, or annotating
6) Don't read to connect, clarify, question, remember, predict, or to evaluate

MALDON'S SCRIPTURE GUIDE: A PRACTICE MANUAL

It may sound silly or pointless to read passively. Well, here are a few benefits to reading passively. Pay close attention to the last benefit:

1) Ensures that the interpreter has access to the scripture
2) Subconsciously triggers your brain to begin tracking images
3) You will begin to familiarize yourself (again subconsciously) with people, places, and things
4) Adds to the overall number of times you read the scripture
5) Improves comfortability with the scripture
6) It prepares the interpreter to ready himself/herself to actively read the scripture (next step)

THOUGTS TO REMEMBER

CHAPTER II: RELATE

Generally speaking, relationships are either horizontal or vertical.

In Chapter I, we read the scripture 'to get through it,' we read it passively. In Chapter II, we read it again. This time, read it actively. The tips in Chapter I were actually a great precursor for how to *actively* read. Let's discuss what active reading is (it is everything that passive reading is not). Literally, review Chapter I's passive reading tips and do the opposite—and you have active reading tips. For example, the first tip was to read without doing a pre-reading analysis or contextualization of the scripture. Here, you are encouraged to read scriptures before the focus scripture (and after the focus scripture). You are also encouraged to absorb as much information as you can to contextualize what you are reading. You are not limited to the Bible. You may access information via the internet, dictionary, or perhaps you will find that a Bible Concordance would be helpful. What relevant information might have an impact on your understanding of what you read? What is the historical time frame, the geographical location and how does the scripture fit within the overall Bible?

The RELATE step is the most significant step in the MSG process. The RELATE step is where the interpreter spends most of his or her time. Take note of as many relationships within the scripture that you can. Relationships can be horizontal or vertical. Identifying the multifaceted relationships within the scripture will ensure the interpreter is able to 1) understand the text, 2) see what's going on in the text 3) gain confidence working with the scripture and 4) it helps to remember the text

All relationships and connections that can be identified are important. Here are some questions to ask yourself while reading the scripture:

a) What are the relationships between the Bible characters?
b) What are the relationships that can be drawn between the people and the time?
c) What are the relationships in terms of where people are situated? Where does the story take place?

d) What is my personal connection (relationship) to this scripture? How does my understanding of its content impact the scriptures target language or meaning transfer?
e) What character can the translator easily connect to? A more technical way of forming a relationship with the text is available to the interpreter by way of **constructed action**. *Many ASL interpreting educators and researchers have examined constructed action. Constructed action serves the purpose of enhancing the message's vividness* (Metzger 1995). *The interpreter takes on, in body language, eye gaze, or in role-play, some character within the text.*

This guide assumes that the interpreter/student has some scriptural knowledge—or he or she is willing to do the work to build that RELAT[E]ionship. Without that relationship to Biblical scripture, translation would be either impossible or replete with errors.

More research is needed, but this guide argues that perhaps more than in a carnal setting, the translator's personal/private life is under the microscope, it impacts meaning for the Deaf consumer. The relationship between the consumer, the setting, and the doctrine is impacted by the translator's own relationship with the faith. Failure to take inventory of one's own faith walk can cause an inadvertent message skew. For example, if the translator appears to be in direct conflict with the scripture (i.e. in appearance, in mannerisms, in behavior, or even in lifestyle-outside of the church) it can cause **message distortion.** Think about social media here. Consumers see what you post. If it does not line up with the teachings of the doctrine, when you stand up to translate, the consumer may not be able to see God because all they can see is you. Therefore, read the scripture again, for a third time. This time, do a personal assessment. Ask yourself, "What is my relationship to this scripture and how might my actions or my life impact perceptions of it?" After taking a personal inventory or self-assessment of how the translator's relationship to the scripture might impact meaning for the consumer, the question is what should the translator do? Here are some options:

1) Continue translating
2) Recuse yourself
3) Make a disclosure statement/disclaimer
4) Ask the consumer what their preference is

We are all humans. We have likely all done something that we are not proud of and if presented with the same situation would act differently. This guide has not been written to cast blame, point fingers, or send anyone on a guilt trip. The goal is to cause the interpreter to think about how they show up in the world and how that might impact meaning for the target language audience.

MALDON'S SCRIPTURE GUIDE: A PRACTICE MANUAL

Hands On

The following activities will help you put relationship-identifying into play. Work with a colleague.

Here are some exercises to practice relationship identifying with any given text:

1) Take pen/paper and sketch out the relationships you see in a scripture. This is called **Discourse Mapping**. Winston (a former professor of Maldon) and Monikowski have written thoroughly about the value Discourse Mapping brings to the interpreting/translating table. Discourse mapping allows students to see relationships within the source text with respect to: content, context, and form (Winston & Monikowski 2000).

2) Students A and B both sit facing away from each other, back-to-back. Student A gets only the scripture (in raw form) on an index card. Student B gets the scripture, but with identified relationships; and an understanding as to where s/he is to see himself or herself in the text. The index cards are taken away from them. Students A and B provide their translation. The onlooking students are to discuss which translation is more substantial, accurate, and produced with more ease.

3) Working with a partner, select either a Bible character or some inanimate object within the scripture. Now without speaking, become (embody) the character. The other teammate's job is to identify with which object, person you have connected.

4) Use index cards. Write out all the relationships you see (use words). Put them in order as they appear in any give passage of scripture, then remembering what those relationships mean to the overall text, translate using the index cards only.

MALDON'S SCRIPTURE GUIDE: A PRACTICE MANUAL

5) Close your eyes, ask a friend to read a scripture. Like a movie unfolding, envision those relationships. Juxtapose yourself in the middle of the scripture somewhere.

THOUGHTS TO REMEMBER

MALDON'S SCRIPTURE GUIDE: A PRACTICE MANUAL

CHAPTER III: RENDER

My father used to say, "Measure twice and cut once." You may have only one time to get it right. Plan, prepare, and produce (I like how that sounds!).

In Chapter I, we read the scripture once (passively). In Chapter II, we read the scripture twice (first, actively and then again through a self-assessment lens). In Chapter III, we read the scripture for a fourth time. This time we read it for an even deeper and more intimate understanding, but also read it for memorization. While working into ASL, plan out your signs. Have an idea as to how you will translate the text when you hear the scripture read aloud. Think back on some of the RELATE activities. For example, use the Map you created of the scripture to translate. This will allow you to break form, let go of the words and to take advantage of your ASL features such as use of spatial markers. It will also allow you to more easily show the identified relationships. Almost intrinsically the Biblical relationships tell a story.

By now, you have read the scripture four times. You do not need to hear the scripture read word-for-word to RENDER it into the target language. By the way, to **RENDER** a message simply means to translate it into the **target language**. Rely on the map you drew and your memory. Here is where you can demonstrate scripture ownership. Ownership means you are confident and that you are comfortable working with the scripture. If you "own" the scripture, you don't have to extend a lot of energy and focus on other aspects of translating. You have memorized and/or know the scripture's meaning and content. Trust yourself.

At-home Exercises:

It is not appropriate to "practice" on consumers who are depending on your translation. Here are some exercises to practice how you will RENDER the source language text into the target language text, before you go to work in a live setting:

1) Rehearse the translation in front of a mirror. Self-assess your work. How do you look? Are you clear?

MALDON'S SCRIPTURE GUIDE: A PRACTICE MANUAL

2) Rehearse with a Deaf friend. Do they have any constructive criticism? What's their feedback?

3) Rehearse with a tape-recorder (working into spoken English) or a video recorder (ASL). Review and assess your work. Allow someone else to review your work. Discuss the product.

4) Ask a more (or as equally) skilled colleague to review your translated rendition. Can they reverse interpret it? Are they able to identify which scripture you have translated?

TRAINING HANDOUT

The training handout on next page clearly shows MSG's three steps (READ, RELATE, & RENDER). The image provides a visual for the interpreter to more succinctly understand that translating a scripture successfully is a journey. Please cite this book and its content (i.e. training handout) as follows:

Maldon, S. (2023). Maldon's Scripture Guide: A Practice Manual. The Maldon Brand. **www.MaldonInterpreting.com**

MALDON'S SCRIPTURE GUIDE: A PRACTICE MANUAL

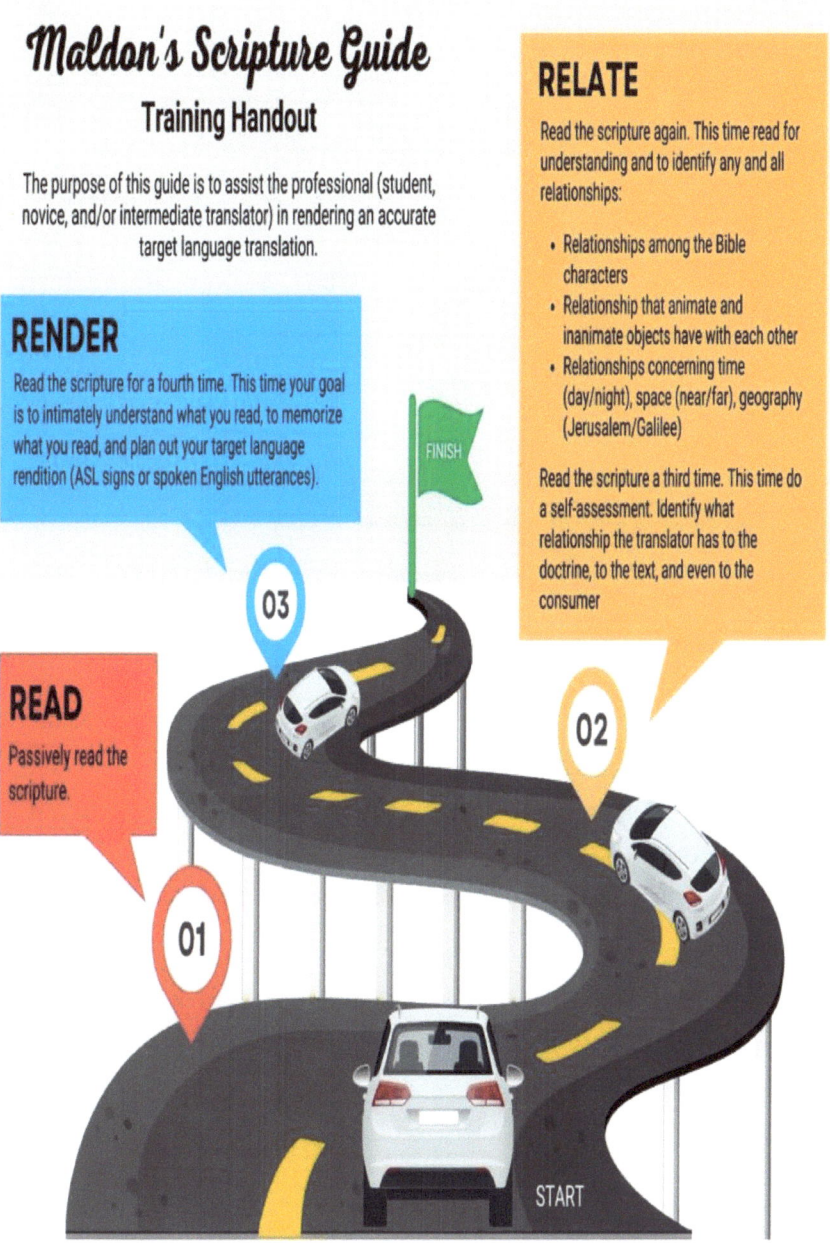

THOUGHTS TO REMEMBER

REFERENCES

Boinis, Gajeski Mickelson Gordon, Krouse, Swabey (1996) Educational Interpreter Skill Development: Grammar

Gonzalez, Roseann, Vasquez, Victoria and Mikkelson, Holly. (1991). Fundamentals of Court Interpretation. Durham, NC: Carolina Academic Press.

Humphrey, Janice. & Alcorn, B.J. (1994). So You Want To Be An Introduction to Sign Language Interpreting. Amarillo, TX: H & H Publishers

Metzger, Melanie (1995) *Constructed dialogue and constructed action in American Sign Language. In Sociolinguistics in Deaf Communities.* Edited by Ceil Lucas. Washington, DC: Gallaudet University Press, pp. 255–71.

Nida, Eugene A. and Taber, Charles R. (1969) *The Theory and Practice of Translation.* Leiden, Netherlands: E.J. Brill.

Russell, D. (2005) *Consecutive and simultaneous interpreting.* In Topics in Signed Language Interpreting: Theory and Practice. Edited by Terry Janzen. Benjamins Translation Library. Pp 135-164

Winston, E. & Monikowski (2000) *Discourse Mapping: Developing Textual Coherence Skills in Interpreters, In Roy, C. (Ed.),* Innovative Practices for Teaching Interpreters. Washington, DC.: Gallaudet University Press

"Interpreting is part art and part science. I can't control the art part, so that means I have to strengthen the science part through avid practice and study."
~Shawn Maldon

MALDON'S SCRIPTURE GUIDE: A PRACTICE MANUAL

www.ingramcontent.com/pod-product-compliance
Lightning Source LLC
Chambersburg PA
CBHW041430300426
44114CB00002B/25